# The Elf Said...

### Notes and Activities to Help Your Elf Encourage
### Good Behavior and Holiday Fun

To my kids
Jameson & Kennedy

# The Elf Said...

As December approaches, so does the arrival of our beloved little friend with the pointy ears, the Elf. Kids everywhere scramble to stay on the "Nice List," but even with the best intentions, following directions isn't always their top priority. Sometimes, they need a nudge from someone who's in direct contact with the North Pole's finest, including Santa Claus himself. Sure, we can remind our kids that the Elf is watching, but let's be honest, how often does that actually work? Whether "no" is their favorite word, you've asked a million times for something to be done, or you're just looking for a way to pry them away from their tablets for a little holiday fun, The Elf Said... is here to help.

It's super simple to use. Just flip through the book and find a note that matches the moment. Got a little one who's hesitant to tidy up? Cut out the matching note, fold or roll it up (see instructions), and place it near the Elf. Then, casually stroll over and say, "It looks like the Elf has a special message from the North Pole!"

These little notes are perfect for the entire month as your Elf spreads holiday cheer and helpful reminders. They're a fun and easy way to keep kids on track, encourage positive behavior, and make room for some quality family time filled with festive activities. Who knew a little help from Santa's sneakiest scout could make the season even brighter?

# Fold or Roll, Place

Each message sheet can easily be folded or rolled up to look like an original work of pixie art. Here are some of the materials you will need:

Option 1: Select your note and carefully cut it out. Fold each of the four corners toward the center and secure them with a small piece of tape.
Festive Touch: Add a miniature bow (optional).

Option 2: Select your note and cut it out. Roll it up like a scroll and secure it with a rubber band.
Festive Touch: Add a piece of ribbon or tinsel (optional).

Quick Method: Select your note and carefully cut it out, no folding needed Place a miniature bow or any small embellishment you have on the decorated side of the note. Place it by your Elf.

Option 1                                    Option 2

"Santa's secret to being bright?
Listening to your parents right!
When you hear and follow through,
The 'Nice List' shines just for you!"

Front

# Contents

"You might find more than one note for some topics... I couldn't pick just one!"

# Listening

"Santa's watching, just a tip:
Listening well keeps you on the 'Nice List' ship!
So hear Mom and Dad and follow through,
Santa loves good kids like you!"

"An elf's advice to stay on track:
Listen closely, no talking back!
Santa loves when you obey,
It keeps you on the 'Nice List' way!"

"Santa's secret to being bright?
Listening to your parents, that's right!
When you hear and follow through,
The 'Nice List' shines just for you!"

"Santa says a star you'll be
When you listen carefully!
Respect your teacher, do your best
That's the way to pass the test!"

"Santa knows a secret, too:
Listening to grandparents is good for you!
They're full of love and stories to share,
So sit and listen, they really care!"

"A message from Mrs. Claus to you:
Listening to Mom is the right thing to do!
It makes her proud and helps you grow,
A little kindness that always shows!"

# Helping & Cleaning Up

"Rudolph leads with a
helping heart,
Guiding Santa on his
start!
Be a helper, just like him,
And let your holiday
spirit brim!"

"Santa says a job well
done,
Helps make Christmas
twice the fun!
Tidy a room or sweep the
floor,
Show your cheer by doing
a chore!"

"Santa's watching, don't you
see?
Helping Mom's the key to
glee!
Lend a hand and spread
some cheer,
It's the nicest time of the
year!"

"Mrs. Claus is Santa's
right hand,
Helping him all through
the land!
This season, lend a helping
hand too,
And feel the joy in all you
do!"

"Elves know the magic of a
tidy place,
They work together
leaving no trace!
Join the fun, clean up
each day,
And keep the mess and
clutter away!"

"Hey there, friend, it's time
to shine!
Let's clean up and make
things fine.
Put each toy back in its
place,
Santa loves a tidy space!"

# Cleaning Up & Chores

"Santa's watching, don't forget,
A tidy room is the best bet!
Pick up your toys, put things away,
And make him proud at the end of the day!"

"The North Pole's calling, here's the scoop:
Santa loves a tidy troop!
Pick up your things, make it neat,
And earn a spot on the 'Nice List' seat!"

"Even elves have tasks to do,
Some are fun, and some aren't too!
But Santa sees your hard work shine,
So tackle that chore it's Christmastime!"

"Not all chores bring cheer your way,
But Santa smiles when you don't delay!
Roll up your sleeves, give it a go,
Hard work brings a special glow!"

"Santa says to add some cheer,
Whistle a tune while chores are near!
A little song will lift your day,
And make the work feel like play!"

"Santa's orders: let's make it fun!
A cheerful chore gets the job done!
Sing a tune or dance around,
Spread some joy while you're homebound!"

6.

"Santa's tip to spread some cheer:
Use your manners all through the year!
A kind 'please' and 'thank you' too,
Keeps you on the Nice List, it's true!"

"Santa's watching while you're at school
Using manners is super cool!
A 'please' and 'thank you' go a long way,
To keep you on the Nice List every day!"

"Santa's watching, it's true indeed,
Kindness and manners are just what we need!
A 'please' and 'thank you' are simple to say,
And help bring magic to each day!"

"The Grinch has changed, he's learned, it's true!
Kind words bring joy to me and you!
A 'please' and 'thank you' show you care,
And fill the season with love to share!"

"The reindeer know, it's tried and true,
Manners matter in all you do!
A kind little phrase goes a long way,
To help bring joy to someone's day!"

"Santa's tip for dinnertime cheer:
Use your manners, loud and clear!
A polite 'please' and a grateful 'thanks'
Keep you high in Santa's ranks!"

# Telling the Truth

"Mrs. Claus says honesty is key,
Tell the truth and let it be!
It shows your heart is kind and bright,
Spreading joy like holiday light!"

"The elves all say, be brave and true,
Always be honest in what you do!
Truth has a sparkle that's bright like a star,
And shows the world how special you are!"

"Santa's elf is honest and clear,
Telling the truth brings holiday cheer!
Be brave, be true in all you say
That's the North Pole way!"

"Rudolph leads with a glowing light,
Because he always does what's right!
Be honest, kind, and brave each day,
And let the truth light up the way!"

"Remember, the Grinch tried to hide the truth,
But honesty brought him joy and youth!
Tell the truth and let it show
It makes your heart grow and glow!"

"Santa's advice, tried and true:
Honesty is the best thing to do!
Tell the truth, both big and small,
It fills your heart with joy for all!"

"Santa's elves loves to give
and share,
Bringing joy with
thoughtful care!
Share like the elves, both
big and small
Kindness is the best gift
of all!"

"Santa's watching while
you're at school
Sharing with friends is
kind and cool!
A little kindness goes a
long way,
Bringing cheer to
everyone's day!"

"Rudolph shares his light
so bright,
Guiding others through
the night.
Be like Rudolph, kind and
fair
Share with friends and
show you care!"

"Santa smiles when friends
all share,
It shows warm hearts
and how much you care!
A simple act of kindness,
big or small,
Spreads Christmas magic
to one and all!"

"Mrs. Claus says it's
thoughtful and sweet
To let your friends have a
little treat!
Sharing toys brings joy
and cheer,
And fills your heart with
love all year!"

"Santa's smiling when he
sees,
Sharing brings such joy
and ease!
A giving heart is pure
delight,
Spreading kindness feels
just right!"

12.

"The Grinch loves snacks,
both fun and quick,
But healthy ones will do
the trick!
Skip the sugar, go for
green,
You'll feel more jolly and
super clean!"

"Santa says to munch with
cheer,
Veggies help you grow
each year!
Eat them up and you will
see,
Strong and healthy you
will be!"

"Santa's secret, tried and
true,
Veggies are so good for
you!
Eat them up to grow up
strong,
You'll be healthy all year
long!"

"The elves eat every bite,
you see,
It gives them strength
and energy!
So follow their lead and
do it too,
A healthy holiday starts
with you!"

"Santa's tip for growing
right,
Finish your dinner every
night!
It gives you strength to
learn and play,
And keeps you feeling
great all day!"

"The reindeer eat their
greens each day,
To fuel their flights and
guide the sleigh!
So munch your veggies,
just like they do,
They'll help you grow
strong and speedy too!"

"Santa says to be brave
and strong,
Take your medicine it
won't take long!
A healthy you brings
Christmas cheer,
So down it goes, my
friend, no fear!"

"The reindeer say, to feel
your best,
Take your medicine and
get some rest!
A little sip helps chase
germs away,
So you're ready to fly,
laugh and play!"

"Santa says, to feel just
right,
Take your medicine day or
night!
A little help to feel our
best,
So we're ready for
holiday zest!"

"Santa's secret to staying
strong?
Take your vitamins all
year long!
A healthy you is full of
cheer,
Ready for Christmas fun
each year!"

"To grow big and strong
like Santa's crew,
Take your vitamins,
they're good for you!
A healthy boost, just one
a day,
Keeps you merry in every
way!"

"Santa says to grow up
right,
Take your vitamins every
night!
A daily boost to help you
play,
And keep you healthy day
by day!"

# Potty Training

"At the North Pole, here's
what's right:
All the elves go potty
without a fight!
Be like an elf, brave and
true
Use the toilet like they
do!"

"Santa's tip for kids so
smart:
Use the potty, it's a great
start!
Just like the elves, be
brave and try,
And soon you'll be soaring
sky-high."

"Santa says potty time is
cool and fun
Every big kid gives it a
run!
Try it out, you'll see it's
true,
The elves all learned, and
so can you!"

"Santa says being a big
kid's grand
Potty training's part of
the plan!
The elves all did it, one by
one
Now it's your turn to join
the fun!"

Santa's helper has a tip
for you:
It's time to try the potty
too!
Big kids do it and you'll
see why,
It's fun and easy, give it a
try!

"Frosty the Snowman's
here to say,
Let's try the potty, start
today!
He may be made of snow
and cheer,
But he knows big kids
potty all year!"

"To shine as bright as holiday lights,
Take a bath to end your nights!
Santa loves when kids are clean,
So scrub up well for that festive gleam!"

"Santa says to stay fresh and clean,
A bath or shower adds a healthy sheen!
Bubbles and fun, don't delay,
Hop in the tub, wash the day away!"

The North Pole's tip to feel your best:
A bath brings warmth and a little rest!
So jump right in, wash away the day,
And keep those Christmas germs at bay!"

"Santa's secret for holiday cheer?
A nice warm bath, cozy and clear!
Hop in the tub, scrub-a-dub fun,
And you'll sparkle bright when you're done!"

"The Grinch skips baths, oh what a sight!
But staying clean is just right!
Take a bath, and you will see,
How fresh and happy you can be!"

"Santa says before you dine,
A quick bath will make you shine!
Fresh and clean for dinner's treat,
Makes the meal feel extra sweet!"

# Brushing Teeth

Santa says to keep them
bright,
Brush those chompers
day and night!
A shiny smile, no stinky
breath,
Or you might scare off an
elf to death!

"Before you settle in for
sleep,
Brush your teeth so they
stay neat!
Santa loves a clean, bright
smile
Sweet dreams, and rest in
style!"

"Good morning, friend!
Here's a tip
Brush those teeth for a
sparkling grin!
Santa loves a clean, bright
smile,
So make it shine in elf-
like style!"

"Santa's reminder before
you sleep:
Brush your teeth for a
smile to keep!
A clean, bright grin is
pure delight
Sweet dreams to you, and
goodnight!"

"Santa's tip to start your
day:
Brush those teeth
without delay!
A fresh, bright smile is
the way to go,
For holiday cheer and a
sparkling glow!"

"Santa says, to keep
smiles bright,
Brush your teeth
morning, noon, and night!
A fresh, clean grin is full
of cheer,
Perfect for this time of
year!"

"The stars are twinkling,
the night is near,
Santa's journey is almost
here.
Close your eyes, lay down
your head,
Dream of magic, now off
to bed!"

"Mrs. Claus says it's time
for bed,
To lay down your sleepy
little head.
Rest your eyes, there's
no need to peep,
The magic grows while
you're fast asleep!"

"Santa's watching, don't
you know?
Off to bed, it's time to go!
Close your eyes and
snuggle tight,
Dream of magic
all through the night!"

"Santa's watching, the
stars are bright
Time to sleep, dear, and
say goodnight!
Close your eyes and rest
your head,
Dream of magic as you
head to bed!"

"Good morning, friend! It's
time to rise,
Santa's watching with
joyful eyes!
A brand new day is here
to start
Wake up, wake up, with a
happy heart!"

"Time to wake, it's school
day fun!
Santa's proud of
everyone.
Up and at 'em, don't be
late
A bright new day is worth
the wait!"

"Rise and shine, it's time for school,
Santa says you're super cool!
Up you go, don't miss the fun,
A day of learning has begun!"

"Good morning, friend! It's time to rise,
Santa's waiting with joyful eyes!
Start your day with cheer and play,
A magical Christmas is on its way!"

"The lights are twinkling, the world is still,
A Christmas nap will fit the bill.
Lay down, dear one, and drift away,
To dream of Santa's Christmas sleigh!"

"Even elves rest during the day,
A little nap brings joy your way!
Close your eyes, it's time to sleep,
Dreams of Christmas magic deep!"

"Even busy elves take a rest,
A little nap will help you feel your best!
Close your eyes and drift away,
Dream of Christmas on its way!"

"Santa's tip for holiday cheer:
A quick little nap will recharge you, dear!
Close your eyes and rest awhile,
Then wake up ready with a smile!"

26.

# Hugs & Kisses

"Santa's hugs are warm
and bright,
They fill the world with
pure delight!
Share a hug, give joy
away
Just like Santa, every
day!"

"Santa says to spread
some cheer,
Give Mom and Dad a hug
so dear!
A little love goes a long
way,
And makes magic every
day!"

"Santa's tip for joy so
true:
Give your grandparents a
hug or two!
A warm embrace shows
love and cheer,
Especially at this time of
year!"

"Spread the love with hugs
today,
Give your loved ones a
squeeze and say,
You mean the world; you
make me shine!'
A simple hug feels so
divine!"

"Santa says to make
Mom's day
Give her a hug and kiss
right away!
A little love is warm and
sweet,
It makes the holidays
complete!"

"Santa's tip to make Dad's
day bright:
Give him a hug and a kiss
tonight!
A little love goes a long
way,
Bringing cheer to his
holiday!"

# Dress Yourself

"Santa's helper has a clue:
Dress yourself, it's fun
to do!
Get ready for school,
look sharp and bright
You'll start the day off
just right!"

"Frosty puts on his hat
and scarf just right,
All by himself, morning
and night!
Be like Frosty, give it a go
Dress yourself from head
to toe!"

"Santa's elves dress on
their own,
Button and zip all alone!
Try it yourself, you'll see
it's fun,
Get dressed and shine like
the North Pole sun!"

"Santa's tip for a great
start:
Pick your clothes and
dress smart!
Just like the elves, every
day
Get ready in your own
special way!"

"The elves all race to start
their day,
They dress real fast, no
time to play!
Join the fun, don't miss
the beat,
With shoes on quick and
socks on feet!"

"Mrs. Claus says, don't be
slow,
Get dressed fast, you're
good to go!
The day's much smoother
when you start right,
With cozy clothes and
smiles so bright!"

"Mrs. Claus reads to us each night,
Stories fill us with delight!
Grab a book and read along
It makes you smart and brain so strong!"

"At the North Pole, we love to read,
Mrs. Claus says it plants a seed!
Open a book and you will find,
A world of magic for your mind!"

"Elves know books are full of fun,
Reading each day makes you number one!
So grab a story, big or small,
And let your imagination have a ball!"

"Santa says, to grow and play,
Open a book every day!
Reading brings knowledge, joy, and cheer
A gift that lasts all through the year!"

"Elves read daily, it's their way,
To learn and grow a little each day!
Every story helps you soar,
Making you smarter than before!"

"Frosty loves a good story to hear,
Reading each day fills him with cheer!
Open a book, just like Frosty does,
And feel the magic, warmth, and fuzz!"

"Elves know the secret, tried and true
Homework first, then fun for you!
Once it's done, you're free to play,
And make the most of your day!"

"Santa says it's smart and fun
Do your homework, then you're done!
Work comes first, then play all day,
That's the North Pole way!"

"Mrs. Claus says, don't delay
Do your homework right away!
Finish up and do your best,
Then enjoy some well-earned rest!"

"Santa knows the smart kids' rule:
Do your homework after school!
Get it done, then have some fun
That's how the 'Nice List' is won!"

"Mrs. Claus says it's wise and cool
To finish homework after school!
Get it done, don't drag your feet,
Then treat yourself to something sweet!"

"Santa's tip for staying cool:
Finish your homework after school!
Just like the elves, get your work done,
Then you're free to have some fun!"

34.

"Elves earn stars by
working hard,
You can too, just stay on
guard!
Focus, study, and do what
it takes,
Good grades are the
magic it makes!"

"Santa's tip for school
success:
Work hard, study, and do
your best!
Good grades come with
effort each day,
And help you shine in
every way!"

"Elves know the secret to
shining bright:
Practice learning every
night!
The more you learn, the
more you'll see,
How fun and exciting
school can be!"

"The Grinch knows a clever
trick:
Studying helps it all stick
quick!
Each fact you learn, each
page you read,
Grows your mind and
plants the seed!"

"Elves work hard and
study too,
It helps them learn and
follow through!
The more you study, the
more you'll see,
Learning leads to victory!"

"Santa says, give learning a
try,
Studying helps you reach
the sky!
Each new fact is a step
ahead,
Bringing knowledge that
will spread!"

"Santa says, let peace take flight,
No need to fuss, no need to fight!
Show kindness to your sister and brother,
And make each day merry with one another!"

"Elves know the magic of friends who care,
Getting along shows love everywhere!
Be kind and joyful in all you do,
And friendship cheer will follow you!"

Santa says, let kindness show,
Getting along helps friendships grow!
Share a smile with your brother dear,
And fill the day with holiday cheer!"

"Elves know the magic of getting along,
It makes you both happy and strong!
Be kind to your brother, share and play,
And make every moment a joyful day!"

"Santa's watching with a smile so wide,
Getting along fills him with pride!
Be kind to your sister, laugh and share,
And spread a little Christmas care!"

"Elves love when siblings get along,
It makes your bond so bright and strong!
Show your sister kindness today,
And make joy part of your holiday!"

"Santa's secret for joy and cheer:
Believe in yourself, hold your dreams near!
You're strong and bright, more than you know,
With self-belief, you'll surely glow!"

"Santa says, don't be a Grinch,
Be kind to all without a flinch!
A friendly heart brings joy and cheer,
Spreading smiles all through the year!"

"Mrs. Claus says with a warm, sweet smile:
A positive heart goes the extra mile!
When you're kind and choose to care,
You spread the magic everywhere!"

"Rudolph shines with a heart so bright,
He stays positive, day and night!
Be like Rudolph, kind and true,
A little cheer lights up all you do!"

"Santa loves a cheerful heart,
Bring positivity to every part!
At school, be kind and bright each day,
And spread some joy the North Pole way!"

"The Grinch once felt a little blue,
But joy and kindness pulled him through!
He learned that smiles are gifts to share,
So spread some love and show you care!"

"Rudolph's teammates all agree,
Kindness is key for you and me!
They lift each other up and shine so bright,
Spreading joy and love, what a wonderful sight!"

"Even the Grinch found a change of heart,
When kindness showed him a brand-new start!
A little love can go a long way,
Just like it did on that Christmas day!"

"Santa's message is simple and clear:
Always be kind to those who are near!
A little kindness can go a long way,
Spreading joy and love every day!"

"Remember, dear friend, as you go along,
Kindness is a gift that makes us strong!
So spread a little cheer, and you will find,
That kindness truly wins every time!"

"In the spirit of the season, let kindness flow,
Be sweet to your loved ones and let your affection show!
A gentle word or a warm embrace,
Can bring so much joy and brighten their space!"

"Remember, Santa is always watching, so be sweet and caring in all that you do,
And spread the holiday cheer, just like the elves do!"

"Get ready for some
holiday fun,
Decorating gingerbread,
one by one!
Add some icing, a candy or
two,
And make a house that's
fun and new!"

"Get crafty this season,
let's make a start,
Creating Christmas cards
straight from the heart!
With love and joy in every
design,
Your heartfelt greetings
will truly shine!"

"Look up, look high, what
can you see?
Clouds shaped like
Christmas just for you
and me!
Let's head outside, let
our imaginations soar,
And find holiday pictures
in the clouds galore!"

"It's time to glide just like
Frosty,
Put on your skates and
feel so frosty!
Grab your friends and
skate with glee,
Twirl and laugh, it's the
best way to be!"

"Santa loves a snowy day
outside,
So let's have fun and take
a ride!
Build a snowman, slide
down a hill,
A snow day adventure
brings laughter and thrill!"

Bundle up tight from head
to toe,
It's time to play out in
the snow!
Make some snowballs,
build a friend,
Let the snowy fun never
end!

44.

"Santa's in town, ready to greet,
Let's meet him in real time, what a treat!
Bring your list and your biggest grin,
This Christmas magic is about to begin!"

"Santa's waiting, don't be late,
Let's visit him online, it's going to be great!
Grab your device and gather near,
The magic of Christmas is almost here!"

"Let's bundle up and hit the street,
To see the holiday lights, oh what a treat!
Grab your family and take a stroll,
The twinkling lights will warm your soul!"

"It's time for a holiday adventure, hooray!
Let's go pick out a Christmas tree today!
Choose one that's tall, green, and bright,
To bring joy and magic to our festive night!"

"Let's hang our stockings, so cozy and neat,
And decorate the tree with joy and sweet treats!
With ribbons and lights that twinkle and shine,
We'll make our home magical and divine!"

"It's hot cocoa time, oh what fun!
With whipped cream and toppings for everyone!
Stir it up, sip it slow,
And let the holiday warmth glow!"

"Gather 'round for a magical treat,
It's Christmas storytime, oh, so sweet!
With tales of cheer and holiday fun,
Let's dive into stories, one by one!"

"Mrs. Claus has stories that sparkle and shine,
Join us for storytime it's cozy and fine!
Snuggle up with a blanket and hot cocoa near,
Let's celebrate Christmas with stories we hold dear!"

"It's time for Christmas storytime, hooray!
Let's gather 'round and read today!
With tales of joy and festive cheer,
We'll make holiday memories year after year!"

"Santa loves a good story, it's true!
So let's read together just me and you!
Snuggle up tight as the pages turn,
With holiday magic in every word you learn!

"Santa's elves love a cozy night,
Watching movies by the twinkling light!
Join the fun, snuggle in tight,
It's holiday movie time tonight!"

"Movie time with Santa and the crew,
Is Mrs. Claus's favorite, too!
Grab a blanket and settle in,
Let the Christmas movie magic begin!"

"Christmas movies, oh
what fun!
Tonight we'll watch them,
every one!
Snuggle up, the time is
right,
Let's enjoy a magical
movie night!"

"Lights, camera, Christmas
cheer!
Our favorite movies are
finally here!
Get comfy and settle in
tight,
For a cozy, festive movie
night!"

"Lights, camera, action,
it's time to play!
Let's create a Christmas
show today!
Dress up as elves,
reindeer, or Santa too,
And put on a performance
just for you!"

"Grab the mic, it's time to
sing,
A family karaoke night is
the best thing!
With holiday songs and
laughter galore,
Let's spread some cheer
and sing out more!"

Ready for a gift wrap
race?
Grab your supplies and
find your space!
Wrap it fast, but make it
neat,
Let's see who can't be
beat!

I've got a fun idea today,
Let's make a gift in a
thoughtful way!
Something sweet for
someone dear
A surprise they'll treasure
year to year!

"Mrs. Claus loves to bake
with cheer,
Making Christmas cookies
this time of year!
With sprinkles and
frosting, oh what a sight,
Roll up your sleeves and
join the delight!"

"The Grinch has a recipe,
oh what a treat!
Crunchy and gooey and
perfectly sweet!
Grab your ingredients,
don't delay,
Let's make some magic
the Grinchy way!"

Grab your apron, give a
cheer,
A jumbo cookie treat is
near!
Santa's favorite, baked
just right,
A Holly Jolly Pizookie
delight!

The kitchen's calling, don't
delay,
It's time to bake the elf-
approved way!
Grab your sticks and don't
you stop,
We're making jolly North
Pole cake pops!

"Let's get festive with a
science twist,
A Christmas experiment
you can't resist!
Try something fun, give it
a go,
Science and holiday magic,
let's go!"

"Let's get crafty and have
some fun,
Making Grinch slime for
everyone!
Green and gooey, it's sure
to delight,
A festive creation that's
out of sight!"

"Let's make something soft and white,
Cloud dough fun will feel just right!
Mix it up and you will see,
A fluffy, squishy treat for me!"

"It's time for a craft adventure, oh what fun!
Head to the dollar store and let's get it done!
Choose some supplies for a holiday delight,
And let your creativity shine so bright!"

"It's craft time, so let's get set,
With holiday fun, you'll never forget!
Grab your materials and let's make a start,
Creating Christmas magic straight from the heart!"

"Get ready for fun, it's a festive day,
A Christmas project is coming your way!
With scissors, glue, and a sprinkle of cheer,
Let's make something magical this time of year!"

"Gather 'round, it's time to begin,
A festive craft to spark your grin!
With creativity flowing, let's make something bright,
Get ready for fun this Christmas night!"

"Santa's workshop is calling, let's join in the fun,
It's time for a craft, let's get it done!
Grab your scissors and colors galore,
Let's create something you'll truly adore!"

54.

"Let's get crafty and full
of cheer,
Time to make ornaments
we'll hold dear!
Paint, glue, sparkle, and
shine,
Create a memory that's
truly divine!"

"A Christmas scavenger
hunt's in store,
Get ready for surprises
galore!
Clues will be hidden, here
and there,
Holiday treasures are
everywhere!"

"Santa says it's time to
play,
A Christmas game to light
your day!
Gather 'round, don't
hesitate,
Let's have some fun and
don't be late!"

"Gather 'round, it's time
to play,
A Christmas game will
brighten the day!
From charades to bingo,
let's have some fun,
With laughter and joy, let
the games be won!"

I told a joke to Mom and
Dad,
One that Santa loves,
it's not too bad!
They said they'd share it
just with you,
Go find them now for a
laugh or two!

"Santa loves to see letters
from you,
Filled with wishes and
dreams that come true!
Write your notes to the
North Pole,
And watch as your
holiday spirit takes a
stroll!"

56.

"I tried to wrap a present… now I'm stuck in tape!"

"I was going to clean up… but then I took a cookie break!"

"Your stuffed animals had a dance party. I was the DJ!"

"Oops! I fell into the marshmallows. Send help (and syrup)!"

"I tried to ride the cat… 0/10, not a fan."

""I wanted to help decorate, but now the toilet paper is festive!"

"Don't blame me for the glitter mess... it followed me home!"

"I started a snowball fight with cotton balls. I won."

"I tried to make breakfast... turns out cereal and ketchup don't mix!"

"I hid in the fridge to chill. Now I'm a popsicle!"

"I tried yoga... I got stuck in the candy cane pose."

"I wrapped myself in your sock. It's my new sleeping bag!"

"I borrowed your toothbrush. My breath smelled like candy canes!"

"I tried to fly with a balloon... and now I'm stuck to the ceiling!"

"I tried to become a burrito... using wrapping paper."

"I asked Alexa to call the North Pole... she sent me to the freezer."

"I put toothpaste on a cookie. Want to try it?"

"I tried to take a bubble bath... in the sink... with whipped cream."

"I made a snowman out of socks... he's missing a head but still festive!"

"I climbed the Christmas tree... got scared... and now I live here."

"I turned your shoes into a hot tub. Your Barbie is loving it."

"I started wrapping the dog. He wasn't into it."

"I made a snow angel on the kitchen counter... in flour. Very festive!"

"I tried to vacuum... but I got sucked into the fun!"

"I made your bed, then unmade it. Much cozier!"

"I set the table with candy canes. Fancy, huh?"

"I climbed inside your backpack. Take me to school with you!"

"I tried to wash dishes. Now there are bubbles... everywhere."

"I rearranged your shoes. They needed a new adventure."

"I got stuck in the laundry basket. Again."

"I'm officially a music producer now. I made beats with mixing bowls and a spoon. Call me Beats By Elf."

"I was dusting... then I discovered how fun sliding on the counter is!"

"I reorganized your closet. Now all the socks are having a sleepover."

"I organized the pantry by snack tastiness level."

"I built a sled out of spoons. It's not street legal."

"I wrapped the dog's tail. It jingles now."

"I tried baking cookies. Let's just say... the smoke alarm works."

"I left hugs made of candy canes. One's just for you!"

"I fluffed your pillow because you're awesome."

"I made a kindness jar, add something nice today!"

"I told your stuffed animals to give extra cuddles. They agreed."

"I straightened your books so they'd feel loved."

"I picked up your crayons so they wouldn't feel stepped on."

"I tried to TP the tree. It's... a new look."

"I added googly eyes to the bananas. They look very surprised."

"I zip-lined across the living room. Ribbon makes a great cable."

"I changed your alarm to jingle bells. You're welcome."

"I replaced your toothpaste with whipped cream. Just kidding! (Or am I?)"

# Holiday Baking Recipe #1

## Santa Baby Cookies

Yeilds 12 cookies.

**For the Cookies:**
3 cups (360 g) all-purpose flour, plus more for rolling
1 tsp baking powder
1/2 tsp kosher salt
1 cup (2 sticks) unsalted butter, softened
1 cup (200 g) granulated sugar
1 large egg
1 tbsp whole milk
1 tsp pure vanilla extract
1/4 tsp almond extract (optional)
Santa head or round cookie cutter

**For the Buttercream Frosting:**
1 1/2 cups (3 sticks) unsalted butter, softened
5 cups (570 g) powdered sugar
3-4 tbsp whole milk
1 tsp pure vanilla extract
Pinch of salt

**Decorating:**
Red food coloring
Red & white sanding sugar
Red and brown mini M&Ms

### For the Cookies:
**Make the Cookie Dough:**
Whisk the flour, baking powder, and salt together.
In another bowl, beat the butter and sugar until light and fluffy.
Add the egg, milk, vanilla, and almond extract (if using). Mix well.
Slowly add the dry ingredients to the wet, mixing just until combined.
Chill dough for at least 30 minutes.

### Shape and Bake:
Preheat oven to 350°F (177°C).
Roll out dough on a floured surface to about ¼ inch thick.
Cut out Santa heads or round shapes.
Place on lined baking sheets and bake for 8-10 minutes, until edges are lightly golden.
Let cool completely.

### Make the Frosting:
Beat the butter until creamy.
Gradually add powdered sugar, alternating with milk, until smooth.
Beat in vanilla and salt.
Separate a small portion of frosting and tint it red with food coloring.

### Decorate:
Get Creative, every Santa is special!
Use white frosting to create Santa's beard.
Red frosting for his hat and nose.
Mini M&Ms for the eyes and mouth.
Add red and white sanding sugar for sparkle.
Let the cookies set, then enjoy your festive treat!

# Holiday Baking Recipe #2

## Grinch Krispie Treats

Yeilds 16 treats.

Ingredients:
8 tbsp unsalted butter (plus extra for greasing the pan)
16 oz mini marshmallows (divided into 6 cups and 2 cups)
1 tsp vanilla extract
1/2 tsp fine sea salt
7 cups crispy rice cereal
Green food coloring (for the "Grinch" color)
Red M&Ms or candy hearts (for decoration)
¼ cup white chocolate (melted)

Prepare the Pan:
Grease a 9x13-inch baking dish with butter or cooking spray.
Melt Butter and Marshmallows:
In a large saucepan over low heat, melt 8 tablespoons butter and 6 cups mini marshmallows, stirring until smooth.
Add Flavor and Color:
Stir in 1 teaspoon vanilla and a pinch of salt. Add green food coloring until it's the shade of "Grinch green" you want.
Mix with Cereal:
Add crispy rice cereal to the marshmallow mixture.
Quickly stir in 2 more cups of mini marshmallows (keep them a little chunky for texture).
Press into the Pan:
Gently press the mixture into the prepared dish with buttered hands or a spatula. Don't press too hard—keep them light!
6. Decorate:
Use melted white chocolate as "glue" to stick red M&Ms or candy hearts on top for a festiv Grinch look.
7. Cool and Serve:
Let the treats set for 30 minutes in the fridge, cut into squares, and enjoy!

# Holiday Baking Recipe #3

## Holly Jolly Pizookie

Yeilds (1) 9-inch round Pizookie

Ingredients:
⅓ cup butter
⅓ cup brown sugar
¼ cup granulated sugar
1 egg yolk
1 tsp vanilla
½ cup + 2 tbsp flour
¼ tsp baking soda
2 tbsp chocolate chips
2 tbsp red & green M&Ms
2 tsp holiday sprinkles

Preheat the Oven:
Preheat oven to 350°F.
Cream Butter and Sugars:
In a bowl, cream softened butter with brown sugar and granulated sugar until light and fluffy.
Add Yolk and Vanilla:
Mix in egg yolk and vanilla extract until smooth.
Stir in Dry Ingredients:
Add flour and baking soda. Stir until just combined. Lastly, add 1 tbsp of chocolate chips and M&Ms, and 1 tsp of sprinkles.
Press into the Pan:
Grease a 9-inch round baking pan and press the dough evenly into the bottom. Top with remaining chocolate chips, M&Ms and sprinkles.
Bake:
Bake for 15-18 minutes, or until edges are golden and center is still soft.
Cool and Serve:
Let cool slightly. Serve warm—best with a scoop of vanilla ice cream on top!

# Holiday Baking Recipe #4

## North Pole Pops

Yeilds 12 cake pops.

**For the Cake:**
¾ cup (79g) cake flour
1 tsp baking powder
¼ tsp salt
¼ cup (57g) unsalted butter, room temp
½ cup (100g) granulated sugar
1 large egg
2 Tbsp (30g) sour cream
1 tsp pure vanilla extract
⅓ cup (80ml) whole milk

**For the Icing:**
½ cup powdered sugar
2 Tbsp (30g) unsalted butter, room temp
½ tsp milk
¼ tsp vanilla extract

**For Decorating:**
1 cup white chocolate (plus extra for red drizzle)
Red food coloring
Green sanding sugar sprinkles
4-6 inch cake pop sticks

**Bake the Cake:**
Preheat oven to 350°F (177°C).
Whisk together cake flour, baking powder, and salt.
In another bowl, cream butter and sugar until light and fluffy.
Add egg, sour cream, vanilla, and milk; mix until just combined.
Fold in dry ingredients gently.
Pour into a greased or lined 8x8 pan and bake for 17-18 minutes. Slightly underbake.

**Make the Icing:**
Mix powdered sugar, butter, milk, and vanilla until smooth.

**Make the Cake Pop Dough:**
While the cake is still hot, transfer it to a mixing bowl.
Add 1 tablespoon of icing and use a hand or stand mixer to beat until the mixture starts to come together. It should be thick, gooey and dough-like.
Note: One tablespoon may be all you need. If too much icing is added, the dough may become too soft and won't hold on the stick.

**Shape the Balls:**
Roll the dough into 1-inch balls and place them on a parchment-lined tray.

**Prep the Chocolate:**
Melt white chocolate on the stovetop or in microwave for 20-second bursts.
Dip one end of each cake pop stick into the chocolate and insert it halfway into each ball.

**Dip the Cake Pops:**
Dip each cake pop into the melted white chocolate and let the excess drip off.

**Decorate:**
Melt an extra ¼ cup of white chocolate, tint it red with food coloring, and place in a zip-top bag. Drizzle red stripes over each pop and sprinkle with green sanding sugar right away.
Let set in the fridge for about 10-15 minutes or on the counter until chocolate hardens. Enjoy

# Holiday Science

## Dancing Candy Cane

### Materials Needed:
Clear cup or bowl
Mini candy canes (whole or broken into smaller pieces)
1-2 tablespoons baking soda
½ cup vinegar
Warm water (optional)

### Instructions:
Place candy canes in the cup.
Add 1-2 tablespoons of baking soda over the candy canes.
Pour in vinegar slowly and watch the fizzing begin!
For extra movement, add a splash of warm water to help dissolve sugar and lighten the candy canes.
Observe the reaction:
The bubbles may lift and move the candy canes around—dancing in the fizz!

### How It Works:
Baking soda and vinegar create carbon dioxide gas bubbles. These bubbles form on the candy canes and lift them up. When the bubbles pop, the candy canes sink, making them wiggle or dance!

## Flying Reindeer Launch

### Materials Needed:
1 balloon
1 long piece of holiday ribbon (thin enough to string through a straw)
1 straw
Tape (double sided or folded over to secure on straw)
2 chairs
Paper, markers/crayons, and scissors

### Instructions:
Draw a reindeer and Santa's sleigh on paper. Color and decorate them however you like, then cut them out to use on your balloon rocket.
Slide a straw onto a long piece of string before tying the string. Then tie each end of the string securely to two chairs across the room from each other. Make sure the string is pulled tight so the straw can glide smoothly.
Blow up the balloon, but do not tie it. Hold the end closed with your fingers.
Tape the balloon to the straw. Then attach your paper reindeer and sleigh to the balloon using tape.
Let go of the balloon and watch your decorated sleigh and reindeer zoom across the room!

### How It Works:
As air escapes from the balloon, it creates thrust, pushing the balloon and your reindeer forward. This is a fun way to see Newton's Third Law of Motion in action!

# Grinch Slime

## Materials Needed:

2/3 cup white Elmer's glue (about 1-2 4oz bottles)
1/2 teaspoon baking soda
1/4 cup water
2 cups shaving cream
2-3 tablespoons contact lens solution
(must contain boric acid and sodium borate for slime magic)
Green food coloring
Green glitter (the more, the better)
A red heart charm or heart confetti
Mixing bowl & measuring spoons/cups
Airtight container or zip-top bag (for storage)

## Instructions:

Mix the Ingredients:
Add the glue to your bowl, this is the Grinchy base of your slime!
Pour in the water and baking soda, then mix well.
Add the shaving cream and stir until fluffy. The more you add, the puffier the slime.
Add Color and Glitter:
Add green food coloring and stir until it looks just like the Grinch!
Mix in lots of green glitter to make it sparkle.
Activate the Slime:
Slowly add contact lens solution, one tablespoon at a time.
It will be sticky at first, just like the Grinch's heart before it grew three sizes!
Knead the Slime:
If it's still overly sticky, add a little more contact solution.
Be careful not to add too much or it might get stiff.
Play, stretch, and squish until the texture feels just right.
The Final Touch:
Press in a red heart charm or heart confetti for that perfect Grinchy touch.
Store the Slime:
Keep your slime fresh in a zip-top bag or airtight container.

# Festive Cloud Dough

## Materials Needed:

1/2 cup white hair conditioner
1 cup cornstarch
Bowl and spoon for mixing
Red and green food coloring (optional, for festive color)
Cookie cutters (Christmas shapes like stars, trees, and snowflakes)
Glitter or sparkles (optional, for decoration)
Airtight container or zip-top bag (for storage)

## Instructions:

**Mix the Ingredients:**
In a bowl, start by mixing the 1/2 cup of white conditioner and 1 cup of cornstarch using a spoon. Stir it together until it's mostly combined.

**Knead the Dough:**
Once the mixture starts to come together, use your hands to knead the dough. Keep kneading until it reaches a thick, dough-like consistency. If the dough is too sticky, add a little more cornstarch. If it's too dry, add a small amount of conditioner.

**Optional: Add Color and Glitter:**
For a festive touch, divide the dough into two parts. Add a few drops of red food coloring to one portion and green food coloring to the other. Knead each piece until the color is fully mixed in. You can also add a little glitter to make the dough sparkly and extra festive!

**Cut Out Shapes:**
Roll out the cloud dough with your hands or use a rolling pin. Use cookie cutters to cut out fun Christmas shapes like stars, Christmas trees, or snowflakes.

**Create Your Own Designs:**
You can also mold the dough into small ornaments, snowmen, or other holiday creations with your hands. This one can get a little messy, but the kids will have some sensory fun!

**Store the Dough:**
Keep your Cloud Dough fresh in a zip-top bag or airtight container.

# Dollar Store Snow Globe

## Materials Needed:

Plastic snow globe (the kind with a screw-on base)
Miniature Christmas tree (found at the dollar store or craft stores)
Faux snow (you can use glitter, fake snow, or cotton)
Hot glue gun (best for this activity, can use other durable glue)

## Instructions:

### Prepare the Plastic Snow Globe:
Clean the plastic snow globe thoroughly, removing any stickers or labels. Make sure it's dry before starting the craft.

### Glue the Miniature Tree:
Take the miniature Christmas tree and use the hot glue gun to attach it to the bottom of the snow globe's base (inside the globe). Be generous with the glue to make sure the tree stays place, and hold it for a few seconds until it sets. Let the glue dry completely.

### Add Faux Snow:
Once the tree is secure, carefully add faux snow around the base of the tree inside the globe. You can use cotton, glitter, or fake snow from a craft store. Pour or sprinkle the snow until covers the bottom and around the tree, leaving some room at the top for shaking.

### Seal the Snow Globe:
After adding the snow, carefully screw the top of the plastic snow globe back onto the base. Make sure it's sealed tightly to prevent any snow from spilling out.

### Shake and Enjoy:
Gently shake the snow globe to see the faux snow swirl around the miniature tree. It's like mini winter wonderland inside a globe!

### Optional: Decorate the Snow Globe:
If you want to add more flair, you can decorate the base of the snow globe with ribbon, stickers, or small holiday-themed embellishments like tiny bows, buttons, or even mini ornaments.

# Christmas Craft #1

## Pine Cone Christmas Tree

### Materials Needed:

Pine cones (you can find them outside or purchase them)
Green paint (acrylic or craft paint)
Glitter, sequins, or small pompoms (for decoration)
Craft glue or hot glue gun
Small star or button (for the top)
Small wooden dowels or craft sticks (for the trunk)
Ribbon or string (optional, for hanging)
Scissors

### Instructions:

**Paint the Pine Cone:**
Paint the scales of the pine cone with green paint to create the look of a Christmas tree. You can paint the entire pine cone or just the tips of the scales, leaving some natural wood color for texture. Let the paint dry completely.

**Decorate the Tree:**
Once the green paint is dry use craft glue to add glitter, sequins, or small pompoms to the pine cone to represent ornaments and lights. You can add as many decorations as you like.

**Add the Tree Top:**
Glue a small star, button, or another ornament to the top of the pine cone to complete the tree

**Make the Trunk:**
Use a small wooden dowel or craft stick to create the tree trunk. Glue it to the bottom of the pine cone.

**Optional: Add a Hanging Ribbon:**
If you'd like to hang the pine cone tree, glue a piece of ribbon or string to the top for easy hanging.

# Christmas Craft #2

## Ugly Christmas Sweater

### Materials Needed:

Cardstock or craft paper (red, green, white, or any color for the sweater)
Markers, crayons, or paint (for decorating)
Glue or tape
Glitter, sequins, or pom-poms (for embellishments)
Ribbon or fabric scraps (for extra decorations)
Scissors
Buttons, beads, or small holiday decorations (optional)
Ugly sweater template (you can print one or draw your own)

### Instructions:

Prepare the Sweater Shape:
Start by drawing or tracing a sweater shape onto the cardstock or craft paper. You can either freehand it or use a printable template to trace the shape.
Cut Out the Sweater:
Once the sweater shape is drawn, carefully cut it out. If you're using a template, you can print it directly on the cardstock.
Design the Sweater:
Now comes the fun part! Decorate the sweater with the most "ugly" and festive designs you can think of. Use markers, crayons, or paint to add patterns like zigzags, squiggly lines, or even Christmas trees and snowflakes.
Add Embellishments & Accents:
Decorate with pom-poms, sequins, glitter, and buttons. Add fabric scraps, ribbons, or holiday shapes like stars and candy canes. Make it as fun and festive as you can!

# Christmas Craft #3

## Popsicle Snowflake

### Materials Needed:

4 popsicle sticks
White paint or white/blue markers
Glue
Glitter, sequins, or gems (optional)
String or ribbon (optional, for hanging)

### Instructions:

Paint the Sticks
Paint all four popsicle sticks white (or light blue for a frosty look). Let them dry completely.
Make the Snowflake Shape:
Lay one stick down vertically.
Glue a second stick horizontally over the first to form a plus sign (+).
Add the remaining two sticks diagonally (like an X) over the center to form a snowflake shape with 8 arms. Let it dry.
Decorate Your Snowflake:
Use glitter, sequins, buttons, or stickers to decorate each "arm" of the snowflake. You can add a gem in the center for sparkle!
Add a String to Hang (Optional):
Cut a small piece of string or ribbon and glue it to the back of one stick to hang it on a wall, door, or tree.

# Christmas Craft #4

## Christmas Tree Garland

### Materials Needed:

Green construction paper or cardstock
Scissors
String or twine
Glue or tape
Markers, stickers, or glitter (for decorating)
Any small embellishments you have laying around the house (for decorating)
Small Christmas tree template (you can print one or draw your own)

### Instructions:

**Cut Out Tree Shapes:**
Start by drawing a simple Christmas tree shape on a piece of green construction paper. You can either freehand it or use a printable template to trace the shape. Cut out several trees to create a garland.

**Decorate the Trees:**
Use markers, stickers, or glitter to decorate each tree. Add ornaments, garlands, or even a star on top (anything you can find to decorate). Let your creativity shine!

**Prepare the Garland:**
Cut a length of string or twine that is long enough to hang where you want your garland to be.

**Attach the Trees:**
Use glue or tape to attach each tree to the string. Space them out evenly or cluster them together for a fun look.

Hang in your house for a cute holiday decoration!

# Ornament Making

## Salt Dough Ornament

### Materials Needed:

1 1/4 cup all-purpose flour
1/2 cup salt
1/2 cup water
Spatula
Mixing bowl
Baking sheet

Parchment paper (optional)
Cookie cutters (holiday shapes)
Straw and toothpick (for making holes)
Paint or markers for decorating
Ribbon or string for hanging

### Instructions:

**Make the Salt Dough:**
In a mixing bowl, combine the flour and salt. Gradually add the water while stirring until a dough forms. If it's too sticky, add a bit more flour.

**Knead the Dough:**
Knead the dough on a clean surface for about 5-10 minutes until it's smooth and pliable. Sprinkle a bit of flour on surface to prevent sticking.

**Roll Out the Dough:**
Roll the dough out to about 1/4 inch thick.

**Cut Out Shapes:**
Use cookie cutters to cut out festive shapes like stars, trees, or snowflakes. Place the cutouts on a baking sheet lined with parchment paper.

**Make Holes for Hanging:**
Use a straw to make a small hole at the top of each ornament for stringing. After each use, clear the dough from the straw with a toothpick.

**Bake the Ornaments:**
Preheat your oven to 250°F (93°C) and bake the ornaments for about 2-3 hours, or until they are hard and completely dry.

**Cool and Decorate:**
Once the ornaments are cool, let the kids paint or decorate them with markers. They can create colorful designs or write names and dates.

**Add String or Ribbon:**
Once decorated, thread ribbon or string through the holes for hanging.

# Christmas Scavenger Hunt

## Items you will need:

Christmas Ornament

 Candy Cane

Holiday Card

 Santa Figure

Christmas Cookie

 Gift Box

Reindeer Decoration

 Snowman Figure

Festive Bow

 Treat or Small Prize

## How to Play:

Hide the Items:
Place each item in its designated spot based on the locations provided.
Read the Clues:
Hand out the first clue, and as they find each item, they can read the next clue
Celebrate:
Let them know their Elf will report back to Santa for a job well done!

# Christmas Scavenger Hunt

**Clue 1:**
"I'm shiny and bright,
I hang on the tree,
Find me up high where
you can see me!"

**Clue 2:**
"Red and white with a
curve so sweet,
Find me where you
might grab a treat!"

**Clue 3:**
"With festive wishes
and holiday delight,
Look for me where
letters take flight!"

**Clue 4:**
"With a jolly red suit
and a snowy white
beard,
Look for me by your
favorite decoration
this year!"

**Clue 5:**
"With frosting or
sprinkles, I'm hard to
beat,
Look on the table for
something sweet!"

**Clue 6:**
"Wrapped in paper and
tied with a bow,
Look for me where
your shoes all go!"

# Christmas Scavenger Hunt

## Clue 7:
"I have a red nose that shines so bright,
Find me where you cuddle in at night!"

## Clue 8:
"Made of snow with a carrot for his nose,
Find me where you hang your clothes!"

## Clue 9:
"I top a gift with sparkle and flair,
Look near the TV, I'm waiting there!"

## Clue 10:
"You've done a great job, now it's time for a treat, find your surprise where you take a seat!"

## Where to hide:

Christmas Ornament – Anywhere on the Christmas tree up high
Candy Cane – Near a cookie jar or a sweets cabinet/closet
Holiday Card – In the mailbox
Santa Figure – By any fun holiday decoration your kids like
Christmas Cookie – The dining room table or where you eat dinner together
Gift Box – Where shoes are taken off or stored
Reindeer Decoration – Kids bed or where they sleep at night
Snowman Figure – Kids closet or where their clothes are stored
Festive Bow – Somewhere near the main television
Treat or Small Prize – This can be a variety of places –
the couch, dinner table seats, etc. (the more searching, the better!)

# Christmas Games

Playing games makes the season even more special, filling your home with laughter and warmth. So, gather around, get ready to play, and let the Christmas fun begin!

### Reindeer Antler Ring Toss
Use a set of reindeer antlers (headband-style or cardboard) and hang rings or hoops made of pipe cleaners or plastic rings. Have kids try to toss the rings onto the antlers, earning points for each successful toss.

### Christmas Cookie Decorating Contest
Set up a station with plain sugar cookies, frosting, sprinkles, and other decorations. Let kids decorate their own cookies and then vote for the most creative or festive designs.

### Holiday Charades
Christmas version of charades where players act out holiday-related words or phrases, like "building a snowman," "opening presents," or "writing a letter to Santa."

### "Santa Says" (Simon Says)
A festive version of "Simon Says." The leader (Santa) gives commands like "Santa says dance like a snowman," and the players must only follow commands that start with "Santa says." If they don't, they're out!

### Reindeer Relay
Have kids race while balancing a ball or balloon between their knees, pretending it's a wobbly snowball or a jiggly sack of gifts. The first team to complete the relay without dropping their "delivery" wins!

### Christmas Word Search
Give kids a Christmas-themed word search with words related to the holidays. They can race against each other or work together to find all the words.

### Decorate the Christmas Tree
Cut out a large tree shape and decorate it with different ornaments (which could be cut out from paper or small objects). Kids race to see who can add the most decorations to the tree in a set amount of time.

### Wrap the Present Relay
Give each team a box, some wrapping paper, and tape. Kids must race to wrap the box as neatly as possible. The first team to finish wrapping wins, but they must also make sure it looks presentable!

### Snowball Fight
Gather some white socks or soft cotton balls (snowballs) and create teams. Kids can throw the snowballs at each other or into a designated target. Set up obstacles or goals for extra fun!

### Christmas Carol Lip Sync Battle
Have kids choose their favorite Christmas carol and perform a lip sync performance for the group. The group can vote for the most entertaining or the most creative performance.

# Christmas Game Ideas Continued

### Snowball Toss

Set up a few buckets or containers at different distances and have kids toss cotton balls or white pin pong balls (as "snowballs") into the containers. For added difficulty, assign different point values based the distance.

### Christmas Tree Relay Race

Divide kids into teams and have them race to put together a "Christmas tree" (using green construction paper cut-outs or stacking cardboard triangles) as quickly as possible. Add ornaments or tinsel as the finishing touch!

### Santa's Sack Relay

Create a relay race where kids must fill a bag (Santa's sack) with wrapped presents or objects. They ra to the other end and pass the sack to the next team member. The team with the most items in their sack at the end wins!

### Jingle Bell Hunt

Hide small jingle bells around a room or outdoor area and have kids search for them. For added fun, th can only use a spoon or a small container to collect the bells, or they can work in teams to find the most bells within a set time limit.

### Christmas Bingo

A festive twist on the traditional bingo game, where players match up Christmas-themed pictures or words on their cards (such as Christmas trees, gifts, reindeer, etc.). This can be a fun, quiet activity fo everyone.

### Christmas Memory Match

Create pairs of Christmas-themed cards (e.g, Santa, presents, snowflakes, etc). Lay them face down an have kids take turns flipping two cards at a time, trying to match the pairs. The player with the most matches wins.

### Pin the Nose on Rudolph

This is a Christmas version of "Pin the Tail on the Donkey." Blindfold the kids and have them try to pin red nose on a picture of Rudolph.

### Holiday Pictionary

Kids draw holiday-related words or phrases, and their teammates try to guess what it is within a tim limit. You can make it more challenging by using Christmas movie titles, songs, or activities.

### Snowman Bowling

Set up a "bowling" game using empty plastic bottles decorated as snowmen. Kids roll a soft ball to try knock them down, scoring points based on how many snowmen they knock over.

### Trim the Tree Toss

Cut out or create a large paper or felt Christmas tree and lay it flat on the ground. Give kids soft "ornament" bean bags or pom-poms and have them stand a few feet back. The goal is to toss and land the ornaments onto the tree. Bonus points if they land on marked spots like stars or presents!

The elves absolutely love to laugh! Their giggles fill the North Pole with cheer, and they know that a good laugh is the secret ingredient to spreading holiday joy. Share these jokes with your loved ones when they need a reason to smile!

Why did Santa go to music school?
To improve his "wrap" skills!

What do you call a snowman with a six-pack?
An abdominal snowman!

Why don't you ever see Santa in a hospital?
Because he has private elf care!

What do you get if you cross a snowman and a dog?
Frostbite!

Why was the turkey at the Christmas party so proud?
Because it was stuffed!

What's the Grinch's favorite game?
Monopoly, because he loves to take everything!

Why did the Christmas tree go to the barber?
It needed a trim!

What do you call a cat on the beach at Christmas?
Sandy Claws!

Why don't you ever see snowmen playing basketball?
They're afraid of the heat!

What's a snowman's favorite breakfast?
Ice Krispies!

Why was the elf feeling so down?
He had low "elf" esteem!

What do you call an elf who sings?
A wrapper!

Why did the Grinch go to the school nurse?
He was feeling a little green!

What kind of ball doesn't bounce?
A snowball!

What's the best Christmas present?
A broken drum—you can't beat it!

What do snowmen call their kids?
Chill-dren!

Why was the snowman looking through the carrots?
He was picking his nose!

What do reindeer hang on their Christmas trees?
Horn-aments!

What did the gingerbread man use to fix his house?
Candy canes!

Why was the Christmas tree so bad at knitting?
It kept dropping its needles!

What do elves post on social media?
Elfies!

Why was the elf always happy?
He was a jolly good fellow!

What do you call Santa when he takes a break?
Santa Pause!

Why did the elf bring a pencil to the party?
To draw some attention!

What do reindeer say before they tell a joke?
This one's going to sleigh you!

Why don't elves use social media?
They already follow Santa!

What do you call a grumpy reindeer?
Rude-olph!

How do elves keep their shoes so clean?
With "toy-let" paper!

# Other Christmas Activites

## Jolly Ideas to Keep the Fun Going!

Track the holidays with an Advent Calendar
Build a blanket fort
Make snow angels (in the snow or at the beach)
Donate extra clothes and toys
Make eggnog
Family coloring/drawing night (Christmas themed)
Do a random act of kindness for someone
Attend a local holiday parade
Camp out under the tree
Sing Christmas Carols
Create Christmas Eve boxes
Make a popcorn garland
Play Christmas I-Spy on the way to family visits
Create a family Christmas playlist
Take a holiday family photo
Attend a Christmas Eve church service
Make festive treats for neighbors
Set goals for the new year
Track Santa
Open one present on Christmas Eve
Take silly Christmas selfies
Play hide the pickle ornament game
Set out cookies and milk for Santa

# Letters to Santa

Cut this out and place with your Elf when it's time for the Letters to Santa activity (note on Pg. 55).

Dear Santa,

Color the back for more fun!

# Magical Reindeer Food

Here's a fun and magical reindeer food recipe.
Perfect for kids to make and sprinkle on Christmas Eve!

### Ingredients:
½ cup dry oats
2 tablespoons holiday sprinkles (red, green, or gold)
1 tablespoon sugar crystals or colored sanding sugar
Optional: 1 tablespoon crushed candy canes or mini marshmallows
1 small clear treat bag or sandwich bag
1 festive ribbon (red, green, or gold)

### Instructions:
Mix oats, sprinkles, and sugar crystals in a bowl until it looks
bright and magical. Scoop into a bag, tie with ribbon, and sprinkle
outside on Christmas Eve to guide Santa's reindeer to your
home!

**MAGICAL REINDEER FOOD**

Sprinkle on your lawn at night,
the moon will make it sparkle
bright. As Santa's reindeer fly
and roam, this treat will guide
them to your home.

Cut this out and add it to your bag of reindeer food!

These festive chores help kids spread cheer around the house, just like the elves! Cut this out and stick it on the fridge to keep little helpers busy all season long.

## Holiday Helper

**Tidy the Toy Zone:** Clean your play area so elves can safely sneak through

**Laundry Launch:** Help load clothes into the washer or fold small items

**Window Wonder:** Wipe windows so Santa has a clear view when flying by

**Pet Care Elf:** Give the dog fresh water or help brush the cat

**Sink Shine:** Help clean the bathroom or kitchen sink

**Tabletop Sparkle:** Wipe off the table after meals or crafts

**Entryway Elf:** Tidy the front steps or shake out the welcome mat

**Firewood Helper:** Help stack or hand over logs for the fireplace (with supervision!)

**Mailbox Elf:** Check the mail and deliver it with a "Ho ho ho!"

**Porch Sweeper:** Sweep leaves or snow off the porch

**Light Patrol:** Help turn off lights when no one's using them, Santa loves energy savers

**Plant Pal:** Water indoor plants so they look festive too

**Snack Time Helper:** Set out snacks for guests or help plate the cookies

**Frame Fixer:** Straighten holiday cards or family photos on the fridge or wall

**Kitchen Assistant:** Stir, pour, or place cupcake liners while baking

**Handy Duster:** Dust shelves, windowsills, or the TV stand

**Santa's Laundry Assistant:** Help fold blankets or Christmas jammies, he loves a tidy pile

**Snow Patrol:** Shovel a small patch of snow or help sprinkle salt on the walkway

**Dish Duty Delight:** Wash or dry dishes, Mrs. Claus would be proud

**Tinsel Tidy-Up:** Help vacuum or pick up after decorating, glitter doesn't clean itself

**Stocking Straightener:** Make sure all the stockings are hung just right

**Wrap It Right:** Help wrap gifts or tidy up the wrapping station

**Table Setter Mission:** Set the table for a festive family meal, don't forget the napkins

**Pet Patrol:** Refill your pet's food or water, Santa loves kind-hearted helpers

**Holiday Hug Helper:** Give someone a big hug today, because kindness is a Christmas chore too

# 24 Days of Christmas Fun

Celebrate the season with a new festive activity each day! These simple and joyful ideas are perfect for adding a little extra cheer to your countdown. Hang it up and let the fun begin!

## 24 Days of Christmas Fun

Day 1: Color a Christmas picture and hang it up

Day 2: Rock your favorite holiday pajamas

Day 3: Sip hot cocoa with marshmallows

Day 4: Watch your favorite Christmas movie

Day 5: Make a Christmas card for someone you love

Day 6: Turn up the music and have a holiday dance party

Day 7: Read a Christmas story under a cozy blanket

Day 8: Cut out paper snowflakes and tape them to the windows

Day 9: Draw a picture of Santa and his reindeer

Day 10: Give a compliment to someone in your house

Day 11: Make a list of people or things you're thankful for

Day 12: Build a blanket fort and pretend you're at the North Pole

Day 13: Do something kind without being asked

Day 14: Wrap a small gift or homemade surprise for a family member

Day 15: Play "Christmas I-Spy" around the house

Day 16: Share your favorite Christmas memory at dinner

Day 17: Sing a Christmas song loud and proud

Day 18: Pretend to be a snowman until someone laughs

Day 19: Count the ornaments on your Christmas tree

Day 20: Bake cookies or decorate a holiday snack

Day 21: Give someone in your family the biggest hug ever

Day 22: Write a note to someone who makes your day brighter

Day 23: Take a silly holiday selfie with your family

Day 24: Set out cookies and milk for Santa
(and reindeer snacks, too!)

Cut this out, roll it up like a scroll, and secure it with a rubber band for a first time Elf experience!

Festive Touch: Add a piece of ribbon or tinsel (optional).

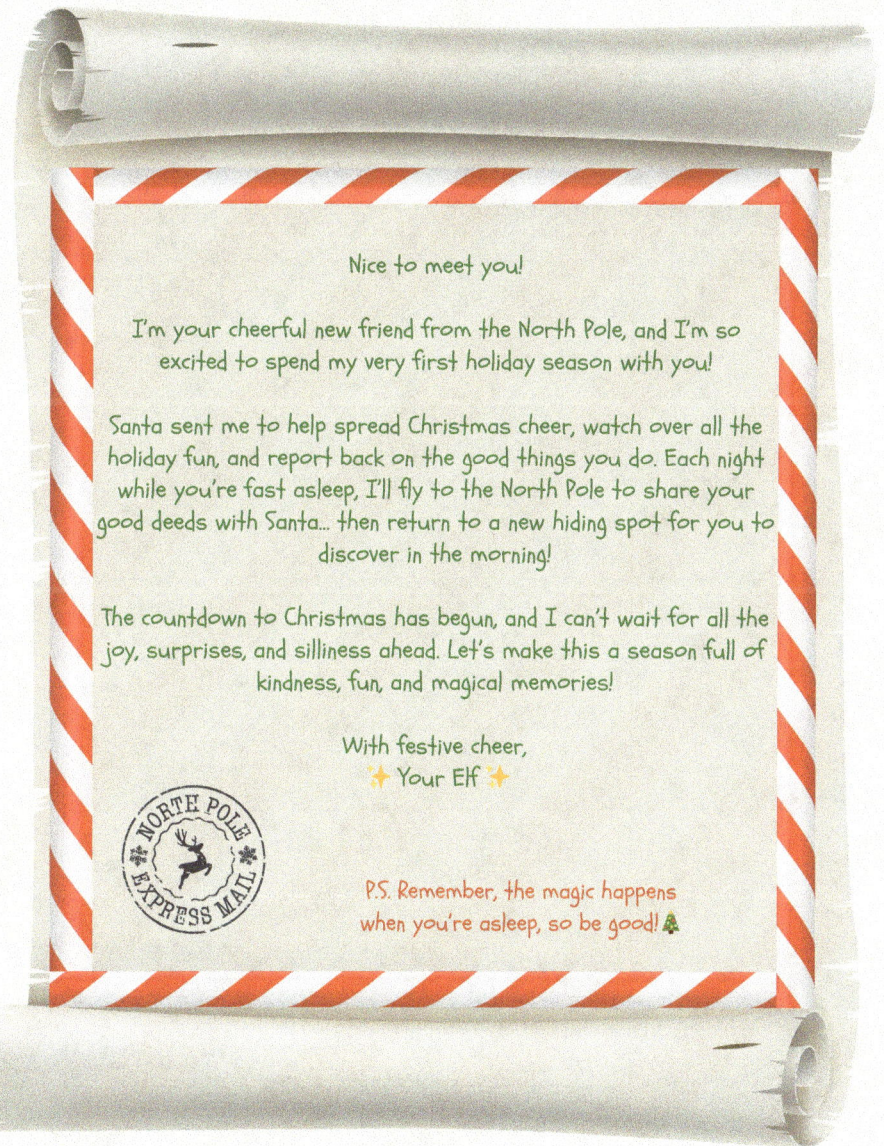

Nice to meet you!

I'm your cheerful new friend from the North Pole, and I'm so excited to spend my very first holiday season with you!

Santa sent me to help spread Christmas cheer, watch over all the holiday fun, and report back on the good things you do. Each night while you're fast asleep, I'll fly to the North Pole to share your good deeds with Santa... then return to a new hiding spot for you to discover in the morning!

The countdown to Christmas has begun, and I can't wait for all the joy, surprises, and silliness ahead. Let's make this a season full of kindness, fun, and magical memories!

With festive cheer,
✨ Your Elf ✨

P.S. Remember, the magic happens when you're asleep, so be good! 🎄

Write in your Elfs' name for a more personalized letter.

Cut this out, roll it up like a scroll, and secure it with a rubber band for a new year, Elf experience!

I'm back!

It's me, your cheerful friend from the North Pole, and I'm so excited to spend another magical holiday season with you! Santa sent me again this year to help spread cheer, keep an eye on all the holiday fun, and report back on the good things you do. Each night while you're fast asleep, I'll fly to the North Pole to share your good deeds with Santa... then return to a brand-new hiding spot for you to find in the morning!

The countdown to Christmas has officially begun, and I can't wait for a season full of joy, surprises, and a little mischief too. Let's make this Christmas even more magical than the last!

With festive cheer,
✨ Your Elf ✨

P.S. Santa's watching, so don't forget to be on your best behavior! 🎄

Write in your Elfs' name for a more personalized letter.

Cut this out, roll it up like a scroll, and secure it with a rubber band to save your Elf from being sent back to the North Pole!

I've been touched!

I have something important to share... I've been touched, and that means I've lost a little bit of my magic for now. Santa always reminds us that Elf magic is strongest when it's respected. So I need your help—please remember not to touch me again.

I know it's tempting, but don't worry! My magic will return soon, and I'll be back to hiding, watching, and reporting to Santa every night. Let's make this Christmas season full of fun, kindness, and lots of respect for Mom and Dad too!

With love,
✨ Your Elf ✨

P.S. The magic is real, and with your help, it will stay strong! 🎄

Write in your Elfs' name for a more personalized letter.

Cut this out, roll it up like a scroll, and secure it with a rubber band to save your Elf from being sent back to the North Pole for good!

Uh-oh... I've been touched again!

That means I've lost a little bit of my magic and can't move right now. I need your help to keep the magic strong...please remember, no touching!

Santa is counting on me to watch over you, and I love being part of all your holiday fun. But to do that, we have to respect the magic. Don't worry, I'll be back to hiding and reporting again soon!

Thanks for understanding,
✨ Your Elf ✨

P.S. Let's keep the magic alive and make this Christmas the best one yet! 🎄

Write in your Elfs' name for a more personalized letter.

# Goodbye Letter

Cut this out, roll it up like a scroll, and secure it with a rubber band for a cheerful Elf send-off!

What a magical holiday season it's been!

It's time for me to head back to the North Pole and share all the wonderful updates with Santa. I'll be back next year for more fun and Christmas cheer!

Thank you for letting me be part of your holiday season. Keep up the good work, and remember, Santa is always watching.

See you next year!

With love and holiday cheer,
✨ Your Elf ✨

P.S. Until next year, keep the magic alive! 🎄

Write in your Elfs' name for a more personalized letter!